MW01627365

Dream Blanket

by Sophie Taylor

illustrated by Danielle Kroll

It's really quite easy to
make your own dreams,

just tell your dream weaver
what you want them to be.

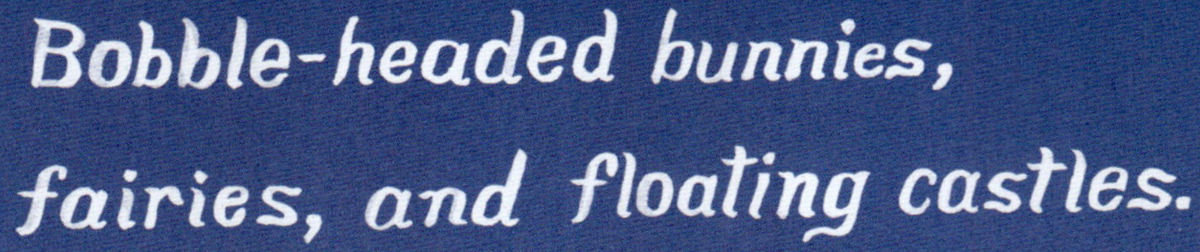

Bobble-headed bunnies,
fairies, and floating castles.

Even a sea made of
butterfly wings,
it's really no hassle.

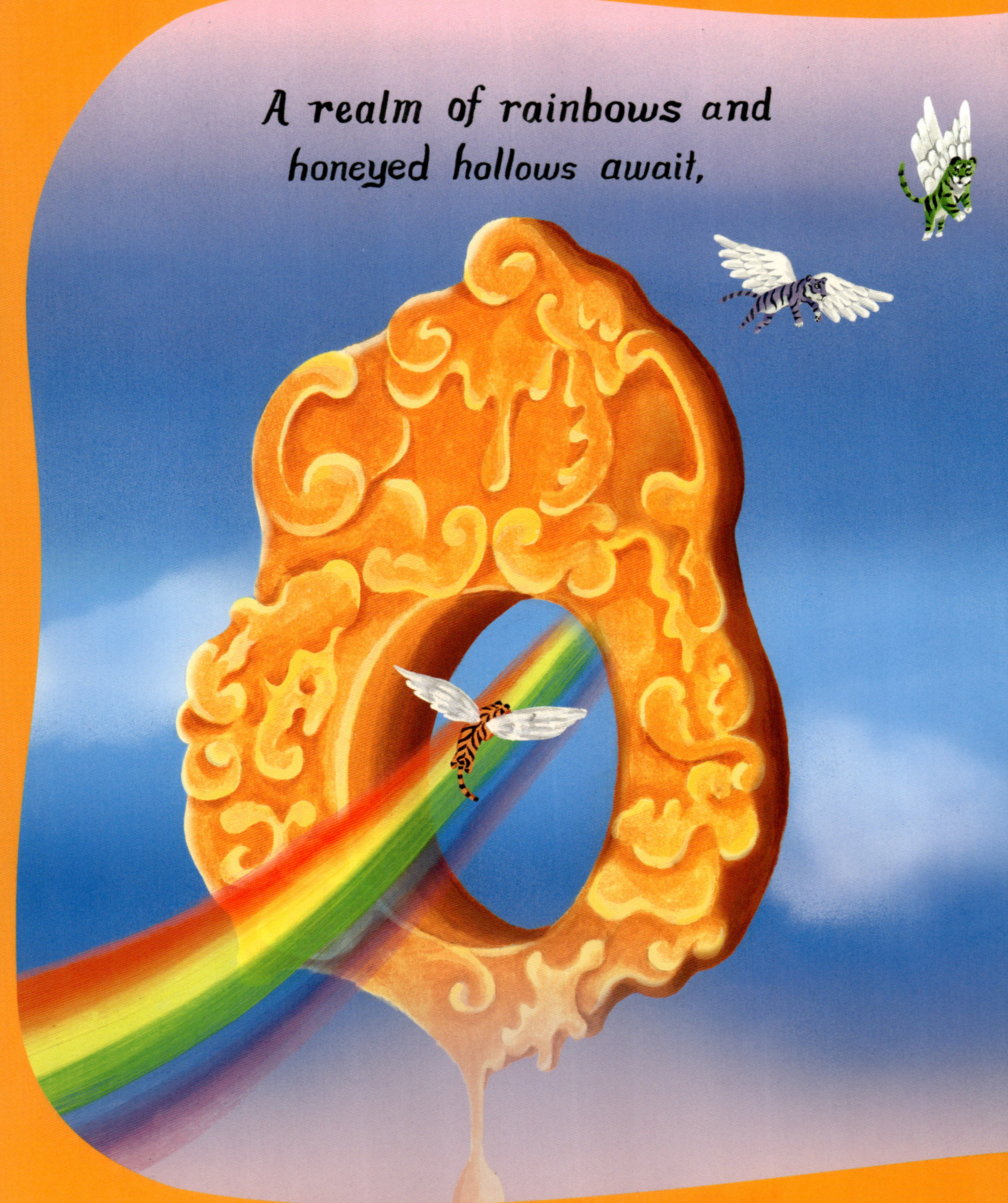
A realm of rainbows and
honeyed hollows await,

with fancy flying tigers
ready to migrate.

Imagine a feline empress
with her Kingdom of Kitties

CATS

or robots that garden
to make their planet pretty.

SOIL
QUALITY

Worlds upon worlds
lie beyond the drift-off mist,

travel there whenever you want,
it's as simple as this:
?

Find the dream weaver,
sometimes she's coy.

Envision her first by closing your eyes.

Once you've got them shut tight,
and you're in a world of shadow...

Ask her kindly,
please
may I dream
of
and wake ready
for tomorrow?

Snickety-snack
goes her big magic loom.
She'll weave threads of your wit
by the light of the moon.

High in her tower, she works
while you count sheep,

delivering your dream blanket
as you drift off to sleep

Write your dream suggestions to the dream weaver here

Dedicated to all the big little dreamers.

Story by Sophie Taylor
Illustrations and layout by Danielle Kroll
Formatting by Brandon Gamm

Hey Moon Press
Hudson, New York

www.heymoonpress.com

Published in 2023 by Hey Moon Press

Hardcover: ISBN 978-1-7374596-9-9
Ebook: ISBN 978-1-7374596-8-2